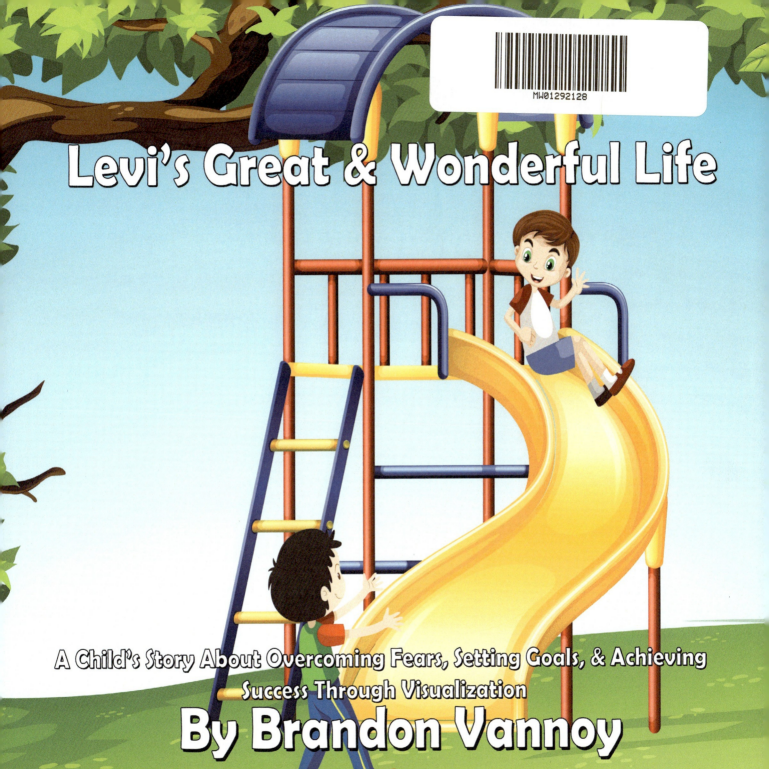

Levi's Great & Wonderful Life

A Child's Story About Overcoming Fears, Setting Goals, & Achieving Success Through Visualization

By Brandon Vannoy

For my son, Levi

It was Levi's big day. Today was the first day of preschool, and mom would be dropping him off soon.

But Levi didn't want to go to preschool.
There would be so many new kids there,
new teachers, new people. It was scary.

"Don't worry, Levi," mom said. "It'll be okay."

So, mom drove Levi to preschool. They drove
up the winding road, past the park, and into
the parking lot. Then mom held Levi's hand.
Up the steps they went. One, by one, by one.

Mom kissed Levi on the cheek, said hello to Mrs. Jameson, and then waved goodbye.

There were so many kids. One, two, three, four... five! More! Levi couldn't count so quickly; they were running, jumping, playing, and shouting. But then Mrs. Jameson clapped her hands, and said, "Okay, everybody, time to calm down."

All day Levi was quiet. He didn't say a word, only to Mrs. Jameson who said, "Are you okay, Levi?" And Levi said, "Yes, I'm okay." But he really wasn't okay; he wished to make friends. Lots of them.

That evening, after Levi came home, mom said to dad, "I think Levi is afraid to speak to the other children."

Dad said, "I was too at his age. It takes a lot of courage. Don't worry, I'll talk to him."

Levi lay in his bed, holding his stuffed dog, Cakey. Dad came in and sat down on the edge of the bed. "Hey, Levi," he said. "I was shy, too, when I was a kid. But you know what helped me?"

"What?" Levi asked.

"This," Dad said, pointing to his head.
"My imagination. Do you remember
the movie we watched yesterday?"

Levi's eyes lit up. "Yeah! *Cars and Dinosaurs Five!*"

"Yep," said dad. "Close your eyes and use your
imagination now to see the movie in your mind."

Levi closed his eyes. Immediately he saw
red race cars zooming alongside T-Rex and
triceratops dinosaurs. "Yeah!" said Levi.

13

"Now imagine something else," said
dad. "Imagine you're watching yourself
on TV and you're at school."

Levi did. He saw himself on the playground.

"Now see yourself with your head up, a smile on your face, and a boy walks up to you."

Watching the TV in his mind, Levi saw a boy walk up to him. "Now imagine," Dad said, "that you become friends with this boy. You start to run on the playground, play with your cars, and slide down the slides."

Levi imagined it all, and it was fun! Levi opened his eyes, hugged dad, and said, "I can't wait for preschool tomorrow!"

The next day at preschool, after Mom waved goodbye, a boy walked up to Levi. Levi, remembering how he saw this moment the night before, said, "Hi, my name is Levi, what's your name?" The boy responded, "I'm Ryan, want to play?" And so they did, just the way Levi had imagined it!

A few years went by and now Levi was in fifth grade. He was on the soccer team and they were going up against the best school in the league. Levi always scored a goal and helped his team win, but today, Levi didn't score, and his team lost. Levi was upset.

"It's not fair," he said. "We can beat them! I know we can!"

That night, dad came to tuck Levi in and sat on the edge of the bed. "I know how it feels," said dad. "I've lost before, too, and it's not a great feeling. Especially when you think you've done your best. Hey, you remember your first day of preschool?"

Levi nodded. "I was shy and you helped me make friends."

"Remember what I said?" Levi shrugged.

"Right here, buddy," said dad, tapping Levi on
the forehead. "This is where winning begins.

Remember, you can see it. Just like how we saw that movie a week ago."

"*Robots Vs. Swamp Aliens*?" said Levi.

Dad nodded. "Imagine yourself in that theater, but instead of robots and swamp aliens, it's you up there on the screen."

Levi sighed, but he closed his eyes. He saw himself and his teammates on the soccer field. But this time, he saw himself and his friend score four goals. Two each. He could hear the cheers of his parents and see himself celebrating with them after the game.

"What'd you see?" asked dad.

Levi told him.

23

Dad smiled. "Here," dad said. "Let's
make it happen. Write that down now."
He handed Levi a small whiteboard.
Levi wrote down:

**I WILL SCORE TWO GOALS
IN MY NEXT GAME.**

"That's it, buddy," said dad. "See
it, commit to it, and do it."

The next soccer game, Levi and his friend, Larsen, scored four goals! Two each! Levi's mom and dad ran down to congratulate him. Levi smiled and said, "Dad, it worked!"

Levi grew up, went to university, played baseball, and went on to medical school. He became a world-famous doctor, publishing books and making discoveries that saved lives.

He also became a father to his own son, James.

One night, as he tucked three-year-old James into bed, Levi said, "I saw you standing there alone on the playground today, buddy."

James smiled and blushed.

Levi grinned and put a hand on James's shoulder. "You know, you remind me of someone. Let me tell you a story my dad told me, and it goes a bit like this: if you can see it first, you can make anything happen!"

James imagined himself on the playground, his head up, his chest out, and stepping forward to say hi to the little boy who walked up to him. The next day, he made it happen for real, and each time James ran into trouble, he'd close his eyes, and imagine a solution.

Levi, too, even though he was successful and accomplished, still closed his eyes and saw how to fix his problems. He still wrote down his goals. And, most important of all, he made those goals happen.

78293755R00022

Made in the USA
Lexington, KY
08 January 2018